UNPARALLELED
LIVING

UNLEASHING THE BEST IN YOU

BY UDI UMONDAK

ISBN I 978-1-7325291-0-6

Library of Congress Control Number
201890777

Printed in the United States of America

Published by Empower Infinity

info@empowerinfinity.com

TABLE OF CONTENTS:

ACKNOWLEDGMENTS

I would like to thank my father for all he has provided while raising me as his son.

A very special acknowledgement to my brother for the encouraging moments and for giving me my first Bible.

I would like to acknowledge and thank my mother for all the love and care she gave while she was here on Earth.

Thank you to all my friends and to the those I consider family, who supported me through the writing of this book: All of you have blessed me in a very significant way.

Thank you to my Lord and Savior, Jesus Christ, who has allowed me to experience true riches in this lifetime through my relationship with Him.

We love to watch and be entertained by the spectacular.

We notice the spectacular in everything, from sporting events to some new piece of technology.

We praise the spectacular; we enjoy the spectacular; we feed off the spectacular.

It provides us with a glimpse of our unique potential.

However, seeking the spectacular should not be our primary goal.

Instead of seeking the spectacular on the outside, we should look for what is spectacular inside of us.

We should cultivate the treasures we find on the inside, so they do not go unnoticed, and so they will allow us to add significant value to the lives around us.

Chapter 1

SEEING THE VALUE IN YOU

Every couple of years, I go on the hunt for a chair to situate in one area of my home. I hope that through this shopping experience, I can find the ideal chair to enjoy in my home.

When I arrive at the furniture store, I go through the progression of what feels right. I go from chair to chair, until… *booyah!* I sit on the winning chair, and I can't be separated from it because what feels right can't be denied.

So, the chair and I coalesce as one, until I tell the salesperson I am ready to move forward with the purchase.

I knew I needed to shop for a chair, and I knew where to get it. However, I still must try out each chair to determine which I value the most. Determining which chair has the most value is a process I have to go through in my shopping experience. Value is sometimes determined by the processes and experiences we encounter in life.

We are in raw form when we come into this world, yet we are created as precious "minerals" given to the rest of humanity. A precious mineral in raw form goes through a process to derive the appropriate functional value for its consumer. For people, the "fleshing" out of your best self is like the mineral process required to bring the highest value to the world around you.

No matter who you are, there is always a measure of contribution to be made if we are aware and utilize the opportunity to be better.

Chapter 2

OVERCOMING YOUR INNER FOES

The impetus for writing this book comes from my own confrontations with complacency, fear, doubt, insecurity, anxiety, and depression. Although I have attained certain accomplishments and sincerely enjoyed countless experiences in my life regarding personal achievement, deep within me, I knew I could do more than I had done, I could be more than I have been to others, and I could give more than I have given. I went through a period in which I felt paralyzed to overcome the mental foes I had to confront to experience and act on a creative breakthrough. It left me in a stagnant and procrastinating state, which produced anxiety

I did not want in my life.

I searched around the world for a better substitute than my best self, but I came up empty.

Sometimes, we live in today like it's a prolonged moment, and yet, tomorrow, there are endless possibilities of change. Applying meaning to our day as if it is a prolonged moment may enhance our perspective on what is valuable to others and ourselves. What are the appropriate thoughts and actions that should be achieved through this moment? Where do we begin, if the present and future are what matter in life?

Ask yourself: What's your twenty right now? Are you in cultivating your craft, shtick or, more generally speaking, yourself? Have you been very fruitful in your accomplishments and experiences, but have more to offer by way of your present and future contributions? Have you experienced the good life, but feel called to something greater and even more amazing? If any of these questions calls to your attention, then this is the right book to continue reading.

Could it be that you have already given up on the things you thought were possible of achieving? Is the light dimming on the hopes and dreams you know you still want to achieve? Maybe you have settled for experiences that are less than satisfactory in areas of your life based on a mindset that prohibits achieving certain outcomes. Are you consistently treading water to survive in the ocean of situations surrounding your life rather than creating a "yacht" of experiences within your life where others can join you? If any of these questions calls to your attention, this book is for you!

I will also provide Bible verses to shed light on what I am sharing with you throughout this book. It will also include the opportunity of a lifetime made available to you, so you can experience some of what I plan to share with you in the upcoming chapters.

Often, throughout our day, we can be so busy, engaged in social media, television, or the lives of those who are not very relevant to our own. With these distractions, we forget we can live vastly abundant lives if we desire them in this very present moment.

At the time of this writing book, It's the summer of 2017, and there are a couple of mega boxing fights coming up over the next couple of months, including a top MMA fighter and undefeated boxer considered to be one of the greatest of all time. Although the fighters might be exciting to watch, none of these match-ups will be the fight of the century. The fight of the century will not be in a ring, on a street corner, or on a battlefield. The fight of the century will be revealed to each one of us throughout our lifetimes.

We have the choice to deliver our best to the world each day or be overcome by a lesser, and possibly more detrimental, alternative. To deliver our best, we must realize how to do so within context. Understanding and self-awareness can assist us with getting on the right path. As the adage says, "Better to be late than never," so we must identify what can be done better or differently to truly enhance our lives.

Chapter 3

EXPERIENCING THE WEALTH IN FREEDOM

In the Western world, wealth is typically determined by the financial strength, power, or net worth of the individual. However, the financial prosperity one encounters only speaks to a fraction of the wealth experience. Many people have great financial wealth but do not enjoy their lives. Some are trapped in the cage of fear; they are prisoners of past accomplishments or current success. The fear of not being able to maintain their image, status, material wealth, and/or identity is connected to those things. It leaves them in a state of rigid experience, regardless of the activity.

True wealth has much more to its composition than financial wealth alone. True wealth is realized by unlocking the wealth we have inside us each day to be a blessing to others. It is the freedom to position our lives in such a way that we become conduits to bless others around us naturally. Wealth becomes inert when it does not enhance the wealth and well-being of others around you. Inner wealth provides an opportunity to enhance the lives of the individuals whom you allow access to and can benefit from your wisdom and help. True wealth should afford the opportunity to help others discover the wealth within them.

Remember:

"The greatest good you can do for another is not just share your riches, but to reveal to him his own."

–Benjamin Disraeli

Chapter 4

ADDING VALUE TO OTHERS AUTHENTICALLY

Merriam Webster's Dictionary defines the word *unparalleled* as: *having no parallel; having no equal or match; unique in kind or quality.*

As Dorothy says in the Wizard of Oz, "There is no place like home." "Home" is where you are being authentic and honest with yourself first; home is also where you are authentic with others. A "good home" is a refuge and an oasis for you; this is where you operate in authenticity and take action on anything that creates fruitful experiences for you and others. As you maximize your full potential in your daily living within your "home", you can create the ideal "home" of experiences, which can far exceed your expectations. Your "home" is your blueprint for living and should withstand trial and adversity. Your experiences will be one of a kind as you work through the process to deliver your best to the world each day.

No one can do exactly what you can do based on what God put inside you. You are unparalleled, unmatched, unique, and authentic. The world awaits your fruitful contribution like the discovery of a distinct hue in a rainbow. Yes, your unique contribution is how legacies are created and it can leave an indelible mark on history. You can impact lives in such a meaningfully positive way that it will provide the opportunity for future generations to glean and be inspired by what you leave behind to connect with their own unique experience.

You are unique in how you are created from the inside-out. You will personify unparalleled living when you allow the best of what is inside you to manifest on the outside. In this way, you add value to yourself and others.

"I praise you because I am fearfully and
wonderfully made;
your works are wonderful,
I know that full well."

–Psalm 139:14 (NIV)

Chapter 5

— ✦ —

UNLEASHING THE BEST IN YOU

Our journey through life has much to do with the choices we make and the paths we choose along the way. Within this book, I will provide essential guidance tools for living to help you experience the best life has to offer—no matter your age, gender, color, nationality, or economic class. It is the secret sauce to making an impact all around you and living fruitfully from the inside-out.

Your potential cannot be maximized nor realized with limiting beliefs.

"Therefore, since we are surrounded by so great a cloud of [witnesses who by faith have testified to the truth of God's absolute faithfulness], stripping off every unnecessary weight and the sin which so easily and cleverly entangles us, let us run with endurance and active persistence the race that is set before us."

–Hebrews 12:1 (AMP)

Have you ever tried to run a race against someone when your stomach is full? An action such as this will not help you obtain victory, especially if the person you are racing against is as fast as you. You need every advantage you can get to win, and this situation would put you at a disadvantage. Consuming and applying the wrong thoughts in your daily living can also produce continuously dismal experiences in the things you have been created to do. Take the wrong thoughts captive, so you don't get captured by the wrong thoughts and actions.

When you allow others, who have limited beliefs about your potential, to influence your thinking, you allow them to partner with you in shaping your outcomes. It is also more likely that you will share common experiences because of this mindset.

When you change your limitations, you can change your outcome and experiences. There are many rooms in the "mansion" of your life that you create. Don't utilize this mansion as if it only has one room; enjoy as many rooms as possible to enjoy its full potential. You will find breakthroughs, new opportunities, and blessings as you maximize your full potential.

"Now to Him who can [carry out His purpose and] do superabundantly more than all that we dare ask or think [infinitely beyond our greatest prayers, hopes, or dreams], according to His power that is at work within us."

–Ephesians 3:20 (AMP)

The only thing that can stop you from realizing the best in yourself is you. You create your own news channel for the world to view. The content you deliver is established by your mindset and the actions that follow. Your mind is a garden to cultivate what you choose to grow and produce.

Sometimes, things happen in life that are beyond our control, but we do have control over how we respond to what happens to us each day. Weeds are evident in the soil of life, as they typically lie dormant. However, we should not promote their growth. We promote weed growth in our mental garden when we focus on the wrong thoughts or cultivate unhealthy, self-defeating, or self-destructive thoughts. A fruit of the unparalleled living experience is flourishing in the peace you have during the storm—or situations or events that are out of your control.

Notice I used the term "flourishing" in the above statement. One of Merriam-Webster's definitions of *flourishing* is *to achieve success or to prosper*. Often, we look on the outside for what success should look like and do not take inventory of what it should look like on the inside. Are you experiencing the peace you need in life based on being the person you need to be regardless of the circumstance?

We must make sure our thoughts and actions line up with what we believe to be true, positively beneficial, and sacred. When we do this, we will experience alignment in our thoughts and actions. We can access the peace we need each day, no matter the storm we are enduring.

Applying a fruitful mindset to life situations allows us to obtain success in what we desire to grow and produce in our own lives and in the world. A fruitful mindset involves not seeing yourself as the prisoner but as a liberator. A fruitful mindset is viewing yourself as one who walks in abundance, rather than one who is destitute. It is identifying and executing as a peacemaker, rather than one who sows discord.

A fruitful mindset is adorned in diligence rather than laziness. The fruitful mindset reflects an oasis of creativity channeled through proper expression. If you are not willing to think differently, then it is likely you will not experience differently. Creativity is not only an artistic expression; it is the fountain of endless solutions.

> *"I can do all things [which He has called me to do] through Him, who strengthens and empowers me [to fulfill His purpose–I am self-sufficient in Christ's sufficiency; I am ready for anything and equal to anything through Him who infuses me with inner strength and confident peace.]"*
>
> –Philippians 4:13 (AMP)

When I was a kid, I used to race my classmates on the playground to see who was the fastest. I continued to appreciate short-distance races while watching the sport of track and field. Experts say that when racing, in your starting position, you need to have your strongest leg planted in front of your other leg, because the longest pull forward is required when you start. When we start off with the day with the right perspective (the strong leg), it can help us pull through the goals, task, objectives, and demands of our day effectively.

Start with a Thankful Heart

1) *Start your day with thankfulness and gratitude.*

   a) It is an essential part of your emotional nutrition and the "healthy fuel" to start your day.

   b) Assess your life. Identify someone or something you are thankful for and verbalize it. As you identify the things you are thankful for, you will also see what you value.

c) Express it to yourself internally, and externally towards others when relevant/ if possible.

2) Embracing Change/Flow in Season

Every day presents plentiful opportunities to make wonderful contributions to the world. We have no control over yesterday, so we might as well focus on delivering our best in the present moment of today. If you are stuck in the past, it can prevent you from seeing the wonderful opportunities in the present moment that could lead you to prosper in the future.

"Teach us to number our days so that we may have a heart of wisdom."

—Psalms 90:12 (NIV)

F.O.G.O: Fear of Getting Old

F.O.G.O can make you do crazy things. It can cause some of us to make very desperate attempts to obtain or retain what was intended to be provided for only a certain season of our lives. The word "fear" is the scrupulous foe of this acronym. So, to overcome this fear, you must reframe your perspective by seeing the opportunity of what there is to gain instead of what may no longer be available to you.

For example, there was a mother pigeon that made her home on the patio of a couple that embraced her every activity. They loved her presence and the noises she would make in the mornings to wake them up each day. They didn't even mind the "clean-up reminders" that she left all over their patio balcony ever so frequently.

Often, the mother pigeon would lay eggs and take care of her babies on this patio, and the young couple enjoyed it, as they loved to see this process transpire in front of them. Then, one day, the couple moved away, and a new tenant moved into the house. They disdained all the activity of the mother pigeon and opted to utilize all possible remedies to rid themselves of the pigeon. The mother pigeon was defiant, standing her ground for the place she called home. The new tenant tried every subtle remedy, but it did not deter the mother bird from coming back, laying eggs, and treating the patio like her home.

Eventually, the new tenant took her eggs as she laid them. He would get her to fly away just for a moment, and then remove the egg she would lay. This action by the new tenant seemed to greatly distress the mother pigeon, and finally, the pigeon realized it was not worth losing her babies in an environment that did not support her expected outcome. Time had changed things, and she had to respond accordingly.

Later, the mother pigeon came back to the patio to lay her eggs and have her babies when the timing was right, and the tenant's mood was more favorable towards her once she arrived in the spring.

The moral of the story is: Do not invest your resources into a place that doesn't support your expected outcome, because you may never see those eggs (your investment) again. If the season changes, you must apply the best methods to achieve what you desire.

Transitions require thoughtful effort; this may mean taking incremental steps toward the change needed to experience a certain reality.

It may also mean taking a few steps back, so you can move forward with the execution of a long-term plan or goal.

It's the aspiring actor who moves from the place they grew up and are well known to the city, where they are unknown, to have a chance to make it big. It is the all-star basketball player who takes a pay cut to join another basketball team, hoping to win a championship. Sacrifice is the ransom for success. Show me someone looking to achieve something great, and I will show you the things they must be willing to give up. It may even mean taking a pay cut to obtain a greater, more significant achievement that you will find more internally rewarding.

Here are the keys to building a supportive environment in which you can achieve certain outcomes:

1) Connect with individuals that support your expected outcome. They say that time solves all problems; this may not always be true, but let time be one of your partners in the vetting process. It is wise to build an inner circle of council that provides helpful insight, advice, or feedback. Make sure these are people who support you and can add value to your experience of achieving a certain outcome.

I enjoy eating a really good burger every now and then, for example. Someone I had a conversation with recommended two places that made good burgers. So, I tried one of his recommendations first. As I walked into the establishment, the server asked me if I wanted something to drink, and I mentioned I wanted to try a certain burger on their menu. I told him I like it prepared medium well to well done. He immediately frowned and said, "We don't make the burger that way, and we strongly recommend you eat it the way we prepare it." I asked him if I could have some basic toppings on the burger, and he responded by saying the toppings that came on the burger are listed on the menu and cannot be modified. I inquired if it was possible to add a topping or two, and by this time, he was really frustrated. He finally gave in and asked how I would like my burger prepared after we went around and around for several minutes.

By this time, I wasn't sure whether he truly wanted to deliver what I had hoped to experience, based on his tone and countenance, so I politely exited and went to the other restaurant recommended by an individual who really knew the burger scene in the area. There, I made the same requests I did at the first restaurant and all were granted except for one, which was not a big deal. The burger was tasty and five dollars less than the burger I was going to order at the first restaurant.

My point behind this story is: Do not let others shape your experience according to what they can't do for you. Partner with people who help you fulfill what you want to experience in your daily life and objectives.

If people don't add value, they do not need to be in your inner circle or council. You do not have all the time in the world to execute what you want to achieve. Calculate your time regarding goals, deadlines, and benchmarks. Make sure that when you are relying on others, they deliver what they promise, so their actions will help you achieve your benchmarks, goals, and deadlines within a measured time frame.

If you cannot rely on these people, then changing who you rely on is necessary until you identify individuals who prove themselves dependable. They say you are only as strong as your weakest link, and unfaithful or unreliable people will prove to be the weakest links in your chain. Reliability is vital to successful execution, so make sure your inner circle of support is dependable, trustworthy, and capable of meeting your expectations based on your needs or objectives.

2) Continue to connect with others in conversations and ideas that support your mission and fuel your journey.

3) Locate places and spaces that inspire you to do your best work and be at your most productive.

4) Utilize all current resources available to you that may infuse you with new insights and help you accomplish what you desire (e.g.; Research, technology, studies, experts, etc.).

Change is the price of admission to life.

Embracing change allows you to blossom in the right season. Sixty will never be the new forty and forty will never be the new twenty. However, there are "new" opportunities that will be made available to you at every age to experience the best each season life has to offer. There can be a laziness or fear of embarking on change for some people. When it is time to change, embrace it, then begin to cultivate something fruitful from the opportunity it brings you.

There are three practical applications to yield a good harvest when it comes to planting crops: (1) Cultivate the soil; (2) Plant the seed; and (3) Nourish and protect what you are growing.

Align your thoughts and actions with the expected outcome. You might not have figured out all the details of what you would like to do for the rest of your life, but no worries. Take it one day at a time. When you get in your car, there is a purpose; you want to get to a certain destination. A developed city offers streets to get you there. You take one turn after another until you arrive at the destination. In the process of driving, you can enjoy the scenery around, you as well as the conversation with those who are traveling with you in the car.

Have a destination each day, wherever that applies to your personal life. This could range anywhere from spending quality time doing something fun with your spouse to spending time with God and reflecting on the things you are thankful for within your life.

Ask yourself this basic question each day: What must I be or do to deliver my best self each day? Then ask: What will be the benefits to implementing and executing of this plan?

Lastly: How will it positively affect others who are connected to me? Completing this daily questionnaire should help establish a more lucid destination for progress. Progress is good, right? Who enjoys idling in their car?

Tap into the Quiet Zone

The "quiet zone" strategy is a technique that will help you identify what is essential to your daily living activities while allowing you to focus on only what is essential for maximum productivity, efficiency, and personal satisfaction.

1) Hear what is essential—ensure that your heart and head align with what really matters by listening correctly.

2) Find peace in what is essential. It will be an internal fortifier. This will allow you to become one with all that is essential in your day, so you

will flow optimally based on your posture and internal focus. Finding peace in what matters in life can provide clarity and a productive flow as you engage in your daily activities. It will help you focus on what is essential and will eliminate worry or anxiety regarding things that do not matter.

3) Be what is essential. Do what is essential. If we don't become and do what we know to be essential, then we will never taste the outcome of being faithful in such an experience. We also leave ourselves devoid of personal peace, power, development, and fulfillment.

"He who cultivates his land will have plenty of bread, But he who follows worthless people and frivolous pursuits will have plenty of poverty."

–Proverbs 28:19 (AMP)

"Many a man proclaims his own loyalty and goodness, But who can find a faithful and trustworthy man?"

—Proverbs 20:6 (AMP)

"I went past the field of a sluggard, past the vineyard of someone who has no sense; thorns had come up everywhere, the ground was covered with weeds, and the stone wall was in ruins. I applied my heart to what I observed and learned a lesson from what I saw: A little sleep, a little slumber, a little folding of the hands to rest– and poverty will come on you like a thief and scarcity like an armed man."

—Proverbs 24:30-34 (NIV)

Identify the unique places of investment that would complement what you have to offer. This is known as the what, how, where, and when:

1) Apply your gifts and talents (what)

2) Give your time (how)

3) Apply it to your milieu or environment (where)

4) Apply it in the present moment—NOW (when)

Don't envy others. Just do you.

Displaced Treasure

You are a planted treasure for the world to see and admire. When you envy others, you uproot your security in who you are for something far less valuable.

> *"A heart of peace gives life to the body,*
> *but envy rots the bones."*
>
> —Proverbs 14:30

Believe and do all that you have been given the opportunity to do. Don't take the shade of others; reflect and bask in your own light. It is not wise to compare yourself with another. We are all uniquely created and uniquely gifted. The combination of the two makes us all extraordinary. Let me say it once again, plain and simple: You have been created for the extraordinary.

Unparalleled Living through Giving

"One person gives freely yet gains even more; another withholds unduly and comes to poverty."

–Proverbs 11:24

When you give genuinely and sincerely, you create a conduit in which you can positively affect others. Giving is the seed that can produce a harvest in the heart if done genuinely and sincerely.

Serving is at the heart of giving. Some of the best leaders in the world have been established through their exemplary servanthood. True servant leadership involves serving others in a way that compels them to follow. You lead by your actions, and that means putting others first. The discipline of servant leadership also requires consistency and availability. You must be present to some degree for a period of time with those you lead, so they have a model to follow. Servant leadership promotes a mutually beneficial relationship experience; it develops and grows the leader as they serve and as they help others to meet their needs.

Four key areas to being fruitful while serving others are:

1) **Be present.** Be fully engaged in the time you dedicate to others and deliver your best as you serve them.

2) **Be consistent.** Always show up and be dependable based on your commitment to those you are serving.

3) **Be authentic.** Be sincere in your words and actions as you serve others.

4) **Put others' needs first.** When you come to serve others, you are not Priority #1. The people you serve are the priority. Let this principle be reflected in your actions and words as you serve them.

Identify people you value or would like to help and sincerely invest what is required to make an impact in their lives.

Resource Potency

I love salsa. I *love* salsa, especially on my eggs. To be very specific, I like really hot salsa, such as habanero salsa. On a scale from 1 to 10, with 10 being the hottest choice for salsa, I would pick the salsa with a rating of ten each time. There is a brand I typically buy that offers a very fiery version of salsa, which tastes amazing with my eggs. Well, one day, I was at a grocery store and I realized they had the brand I preferred but not the flavor. I decided to try the mild version and see how it went with my eggs. As I tried the milder flavor of salsa, I realized the simple beauty of my preferred habanero flavor. I found I had to use more salsa for my eggs with the milder flavor. The potency to deliver a hot experience in the habanero salsa far exceeded the milder flavor.

The takeaway from this example is threefold: First, make sure you are cultivating your gifts so that when you apply them to the right environment, there is a potent, positive impact. Second, quality precedes quantity. A bundle of half-hearted actions may never measure up to one genuine act of love. Third, be discerning about where you apply yourself as a resource to invest.

> *"Cast your bread on the surface of the waters [be diligently active, make thoughtful decisions], for you will find it after many days."*
>
> *—Ecclesiastes 11:1 (AMP)*

Quality should always be in surplus. Make sure you are implementing and executing the 3T Strategy. The 3T Strategy helps you adopt the right tools, technology, and techniques to help ensure your success and effectiveness in the related season. Do not let complacency or apathy leave you stymied in realizing what is required of you to perform at your best.

> *"If the ax is dull*
> *and its edge unsharpened,*
> *more strength is needed,*
> *but skill will bring success."*

> –Ecclesiastes 10:10 (NIV)

The blessing or satisfaction of giving comes by way of the opportunity and is not limited to the outcome. It is wise to steward your time and resources with expectations or hope of successful outcomes, but you will not always see the harvest or outcome in every giving opportunity.

There are exponential effects of giving. Your giving can have such an impact. It can stir others to implement the act of giving, creating a prolific activity of giving within a group, family, community, or organization.

Maximizing the Talents and Gifts You Have Been Given

Leave no stone unturned with the gifts and talents you offer to serve as an added value to those around you. Identify which talents and gifts complement your season and environment, then engage them accordingly.

If money was not an option, how would you spend your time? How would you like to add value to others around you, in your community, or around the world? There is inner peace that comes from knowing what you should do and doing it rather than not doing it all and feeling guilty, sad, or confused.

There are four essential elements to help you maximize your gifts and talents. These critical building blocks are: (1) Understanding; (2) Vision; (3) Execution; and (4) Discipline.

1) Understanding: Facing Challenges and Trials

"It is better to go to a house of mourning
than to go to a house of feasting,
for death is the destiny of everyone;
the living should take this to heart."

–Ecclesiastes 7:2 (NIV)

There is a silver lining in the trials, challenges, and adversities we encounter. They offer us opportunities to ponder their meaning, which may prove cathartic. It may help us gain further insight into an experience or situation, or it may illuminate significance in some area of our lives in the presence of the challenges we face. Without these tougher moments in life, we may not take the time to reflect and gather these gems of understanding indirectly as we go through the process of a certain trial.

Understanding can also trigger your "reason for the season." Understanding always helps you "reroute" back to your purpose, the big picture, or the central theme of your life. Understanding helps you define your purpose and creates lucidity in your thinking, so you can use your time and resources wisely on the right things and for the right people. You wouldn't buy $1,000 worth of sports equipment for a sport you don't plan to play or do not enjoy. That example may sound ludicrous, but many make foolish choices like this in relationships, business, and other areas of their lives. Understanding is the telescope that allows you to see the stars within yourself; it serves as a guard and protector of your destiny and purpose.

*"Discretion will watch over you.
Understanding and discernment will
guard you."*

—Proverbs 2:11

2) Vision: Anchored by Understanding

Vision is composed of the details, plans, and actions you will take to be fruitful in your life. A forecast and metric for your vision can be broken down from annually to hourly. Vision is your blueprint for constructing the ideal home within yourself.

3) Execution

"The sluggard is wiser in his own eyes than seven men who can answer sensibly."

—Proverbs 26:16

Sometimes, the biggest obstacle is just getting started. Delays, setbacks, and excuses all play a role in hindering your progress and momentum.

"He who watches the wind [waiting for all conditions to be perfect] will not sow [a seed], and he who looks at the clouds will not reap [a harvest]."

–Ecclesiastes 11:4 (AMP)

You must be your own biggest and best accountability partner by doing what you say you will do. Write or type you vision, plans, and action steps out so that you can be held accountable to faithfully following your path of execution. Focus on these objectives until the completion of your goal is accomplished.

Having an applied focus on your craft, objectives, and goals is very crucial for the following reasons:

a) You can take advantage of ideas, concept, strategies, and solutions that only become present when you are mentally present, available, and one with your objectives–not divided by other distractions. Applying a dedicated focus allows you to see what you must, so you can deliver what you must.

b) Compound learning: you can enhance your gifting or skill-set by adding to what you already know to cultivate new methods, concepts, technologies, and protocols. A dedicated focus towards the object or goal allows time for compound learning to take place more rapidly.

c) Applying an unwavering focus on what you must do will assist in eliminating what is unnecessary to help you accomplish your goal. Focus is the vitamin tablet or superfood with all the nutrients you need to stay on the healthy path to obtaining your goal. Focus only on what is needed and essential. Be the CEO of your own domain: Implement a good process in your environment; fire unhealthy habits and lay off unsupportive relationships. You liberate and emancipate the gifts within you when you create based on your calling or craft. What you create should employ the resources to sustain you, and eventually, allow you to thrive.

4) Discipline

I love to work out. I enjoy sprinting, HIIT training, and weightlifting. One significant benefit to weightlifting is building muscle. It requires lifting repetitively with weights to foster muscle growth. This requires consistency within an appropriate workout plan or strategy.

Discipline means consistently executing on the appropriate action to develop or "grow" the muscle you desire for your expected outcome.

Understanding, Vision, Execution, and **Discipline** are the four key traits.

Gaining personal understanding of what is driving you to do anything of significance is highly important. Understanding is the telescope which allows you to see the stars in your head and heart.

Getting Clarity

Clarity helps address the who, what, when, where, and how. It also allows you to put the focus on the right areas.

Your faithfulness in applying your gifts and talents will open new doors of opportunity.

"A man's gift will make room for him in the presence of great men."

—Proverbs 18:16

"Do you see a man skillful and experienced in his work?

*He will stand [in honor] before kings;
He will not stand before obscure men."*

—Proverbs 22:29 (AMP)

Act where action is required. Regret is the residue of destiny and purpose unfulfilled. Hope deferred makes the heart sick. The poet, Henry David Thoreau, provided a similar thought when he said, *"Many men live lives of quiet desperation."*

Prospering in the Abundance of Love Toward Others

If you are going to live a life worth living, then love is essential. Love others in such a way that there will never be another opportunity like it to give yourself sincerely to that person. Scarce water is very precious and essential in very dry land. Water is a precious resource in a dry environment, and so is the love needed in any relationship. Let your actions confirm or reiterate your words when it comes to loving others. Identify the best way to love them based on who they are and what loves means to them. Understand the importance of love-mapping and love languages by John Guttman and Gary Smalley, respectively. You can read both of their books on these subjects and see how they may apply to loving others.

Never Forget to Forgive Yourself

Forgive yourself. Start every day with a new slate.

There is a mental, emotional, and spiritual currency you can access to bring your "A" game and deliver your best each day. It's available twenty-four hours a day, and you have the option to use it or not. If someone gave you access to ten million dollars and said, "Spend it on everything that will benefit you and your loved ones within twenty-four hours, or lose it," would you access it and spend it wisely?

Not forgiving is the exact opposite scenario. It's like magnifying a debt from the past that you feel is owed to you. It need not be an outstanding debt when it comes to your life in the present. It is up to you to make the best choice that will bring the most benefit to you and those you come across in your lifetime.

Access the mental, emotional, and spiritual currency you need to forgive yourself in a situation or relationship so that you will be free to experience all that each new day has to offer with no emotional encumbrances based on your past. Forgiveness is inexpensive self-therapy.

How to Cultivate Authenticity from the Inside-Out

Be honest with yourself. Know thyself.

Authenticity begins when you are honest with yourself first. Then your outward expression will reflect and connect with others in a genuine way. It requires deciphering what's working and what's not working in your life. Authenticity demands that we own up to what hurts us, what makes us feel good, and even the things that test our patience and our nerves.

In commercial real estate, it is common for a landlord to deliver a rental space clean and unfurnished to the new tenant unless stated in the advertising or lease agreement. Sometimes, there are certain articles, items, or trash left behind by the previous tenant that the new tenants encounter in the space as they move in. It is the new tenant's duty to furnish and decorate the space in such a way that they can work well within it and thrive.

Often, we go through things in our past, such as disappointment; that disappointment leads us to leave certain rooms in our lives empty or with items that no longer belong there. We are in the present and it is filled with opportunity. You must be honest with yourself about any obstacle in your life that is preventing you from decorating or furnishing your life in the way you see fit and the way you ideally imagine. From there, plan and act accordingly. Don't waver. Just focus on the plan and the action that follows. Fill that space or area of your life with things you want to see and experience, and this is where you become the Picasso of your life. Make what you create something you enjoy because you are being true to yourself first.

Being honest with yourself requires acknowledging past, present, and future expectations. Give yourself a window to see and assess progress or see where change is needed.

How to Address Unavoidable Pain

There will be times when we encounter pain that is unavoidable. A good example is losing a loved one. When pain you can't avoid comes to your doorstep, welcome it into your house of good health. Allowing pain to have time with you can prove to be beneficial. There are moments when you must become one with pain. This coalescence allows you to see pain's role in the process of revealing to healing. This is a time for connection, when you and pain can have a candid exchange with one another. Through your conversation, pain may reveal things you didn't know or need to know about yourself. Sometimes, it just wants to make its presence known and it wants you to embrace it as a part of your journey in life.

Like any good host, you will politely say good night and usher it out your front door when you have had its company for too long. God will provide you with the wisdom to know it is time for pain to leave your doorstep. Prematurely dismissing pain or ignoring pain can have dire consequences. Pain is like the FedEx delivery you have to sign for because the contents of the package are intended just for you and no one else. Take it. Sign it and embrace the contents, then see what the experience reveals to you. Again, this is applicable specifically when you experience pain you can't avoid as you pursue healthy outcomes, or when you are experiencing trial or suffering.

Allow yourself to connect with and relate to others in a genuine way. Your story and testimony can connect when you are genuinely and transparently connected to you. Know thyself.

Respect and value yourself. Do not let anything or anyone make you feel less than what you know you are worth. Sometimes, you may feel slighted when others have rejected you, disregarded you, or have not taken you seriously. These experiences can be of immense value. They are an opportunity to thank the situation or the person for providing the added definition to your purpose and destiny. It should establish a more secure foundation in who you are, rather than create insecurity based on their actions or behavior towards you.

Allow healthy accountability to support you in your purpose and with your goals. Denying responsibility hinders the opportunity to get help, insight, or counsel from others when you need it.

"Real love does not withhold truth. Open rebuke is better than secret love."

–Proverbs 25:7

"Each heart knows its own bitterness and no one else can share it in its joy."

–Proverbs 14:10

Finding Rewards Through Healthy Curiosity

Add a dose of healthy curiosity to your lifestyle. Pursue and explore what engages your sense of curiosity, if it is healthy and will benefit your life and your purpose here on Earth.

> *"It is the glory of God to conceal a matter; to search out a matter is the glory of kings."*
>
> *–Proverbs 25:2 (NIV)*

> *"The purposes of a person's heart are deep waters, but one who has insight draws them out."*
>
> *–Proverbs 20:5 (NIV)*

> *"Test all things. Hold fast to what is good."*
>
> *–First Thessalonians 5:21 (NKJV)*

Allow others you respect and trust to provide opportunities to enlarge your understanding experiences.

How to Make Room for What Captivates You

Stay in awe. Don't make much of things that really don't matter or miss capturing the blessings in front of you. Simplicity can be the remedy for moments of chaos, stress, or distraction. When tasks or commitments become too much to handle, it may be wise to simplify. Maybe everything you have put on your plate can be separated by priority and can be done over time, so you must provide yourself time to rest, relax, or take a break. There is more to life than what we can see, hear, smell, feel, and touch. We are a modicum of all that has been created on the Earth, yet we have such significance to the world in which we have been given the responsibility to steward.

This understanding should invoke a sense of humility and awe for the privileges that have been granted to us while we live on Earth.

Enjoy your life; this is a privilege given to you by your Creator. There is a time and a season for everything. Take time to rest and enjoy the blessings in your life.

> *"One hand full of rest and patience is better than two fists full of labor and chasing after the wind."*
>
> —Ecclesiastes 4:6 (AMP)

Time is a precious resource, and we must use it wisely.

> *"There is a season (a time appointed) for everything and a time for every delight and event or purpose under heaven."*
>
> —Ecclesiastes 3:1 (AMP)

Distraction is not your friend. Consider it to be the temptress or devious seducer that wants to keep you away from those whom you need to stay faithful to. Shouldn't you invest quality time in cultivating your craft, rather than spend a majority of your time engaged in idle activity online? It might be more valuable to spend more time with a loved one, rather than be heavily engaged in activities of minimal significance. It may be better to volunteer your time helping others instead of seeking out an absorbent amount of entertainment elsewhere. Only you will know, as you do a reality check of the daily choices you are making, what kind of help you can offer in the best ways possible or what prevents you from doing so.

"Making the very most of your time [on Earth, recognizing and taking advantage of each opportunity and using it with

wisdom and diligence], because the days are [filled with] evil."

—Ephesians 5:16 (AMP)

It is beneficial to have a posture that allows you to be open to growth and enrichment from new opportunities throughout life. It's okay to not have all the answers to everything. Some things may get figured out and some things, we may never know. Take the time to be present and realize just how magnificent the opportunity is to work, rest, play, and enjoy your surroundings and the people in your life.

"The Lord is my Shepherd [to feed, to guide, and to shield me],
I shall not want.
He lets me lie down in green pastures;
He leads me beside the still and quiet waters.
He refreshes and restores my soul [life];

He leads me in the paths of righteousness
for His name's sake.
Even though I walk through the [sunless] valley
of the shadow of death,
I fear no evil, for You are with me;
Your rod [to protect] and Your staff [to guide],
they comfort and console me.
You prepare a table before me in the presence
of my enemies.
You have anointed and refreshed my head
with oil;
My cup overflows.
Surely, goodness and mercy and unfailing love
shall follow me all the days of my life,
And I shall dwell forever [throughout all my
days] in the house and in the presence of the
Lord."

—Psalm 23 (AMP)

Rest is necessary. Rest invigorates us for our next episode of purposeful activity. Rest should provide a replenishment or infusion we need most, which any degree of work cannot deliver. You can be lying down but not resting from your thoughts. This is where the body and mind must find congruency, so the maximum benefits can be achieved through rest and relaxation.

Abundance transcends the temporal; the present is connected to the eternal.

Let's say you have a full carton of juice and an empty glass. You can only fill the glass to its limit, yet more juice remains in the carton. Let's say I happen to know the juice maker who has an unlimited supply of fruit to make the juice. I could introduce you to the juice maker and he could tailor-make the juice perfect for your palate that no other juice could ever compare to. Would you want to meet the juice maker, and would you want to taste the juice he intended for you to enjoy?

The Opportunity of a Lifetime: Access the Best Eternity Has to Offer

If you are reading this book, I am sure you are seeking to live the best life you can live in the present, but I would encourage you to take advantage of the best that eternity has to offer by coming into a relationship with Jesus Christ as your Lord and Savior. No matter how sweet or difficult life has been up until now, we can access the heavenly authority, power, and wisdom that comes from being in a relationship with Jesus Christ, and by the Holy Spirit who intercedes for us. We can never live full and abundant lives without Jesus, regardless of the way things may appear because of sin. Jesus Christ died on the cross and paid the penalty for all our sins. Through Him, we can have a relationship with God the Father and the opportunity to live a truly abundant life!

"For physical training is of some value, but godliness has value for all things, holding promise for both the present life and the life that is to come."

−1 Timothy 4:8 (NIV)

"But godliness actually is a source of great gain when accompanied by contentment [that contentment which comes from a sense of inner confidence based on the sufficiency of God]."

−1 Timothy 6:6 (AMP)

Once you come into a relationship with Jesus, your sufficiency comes from being in a relationship with Him. When He becomes the center of your life, He fills us with what we need, so we can find true contentment in God, and God alone. It becomes a matter not so much of what is in your life, but who is in your life. God will provide you with the peace you need and will be your provider.

The apostle Paul had grasped the secret sauce to contentment in his own life experience.

"I know what it is to be in need, and I know what it is to have plenty. I have learned the secret of being content in any and every situation, whether well-fed or hungry, whether living in plenty or in want. I can do all this through Him, who gives me strength."

–Philippians 4:12-13 (NIV)

A personal relationship with Jesus allows you to live in eternal abundance *now*. You can have access to God's power, wisdom, heavenly authority, and love to experience the abundant life from now to eternity. The personal relationship with Jesus is the opportunity of a lifetime that will affect what will be made available to you for eternity.

The scripture below reiterates this point:

> *"The thief comes only in order to steal and kill and destroy. I came that they may have and enjoy life, and have it in abundance [to the fullest, 'til it overflows]."*
>
> –John 10:10 (AMP)

A relationship with Jesus is the only way to come into the eternal life of abundance, and only through Him alone can we access it. Not only will we have it for ourselves, but we will have the capacity of this living abundance overflowing through us. Others around you can be affected by the light in you (Jesus powered by the Holy Spirit). They will come into the light and access the abundant life for themselves, as they accept Christ as their Lord and Savior.

You may feel ambivalent about what I am sharing with you now. This may require going down a new path that will affect the rest of your life. Do not let the fear of the unknown paralyze you from obtaining all that is in store for your life as you come into a relationship with Jesus. As the saying goes, "nothing ventured, nothing gained". This is not something that can just be conceptualized; it is far better realized as you walk with Him. You must decide to follow Jesus to experience the joy and blessings He has in store for you.

Man reaches for some of the pleasures of eternity, but he falls short of their grasp without

God. The good news is that eternal pleasures and riches are available and accessible through a relationship with Jesus.

> *"For to the person who pleases Him, God gives wisdom, knowledge, and joy; but to the sinner, He gives the work of gathering and collecting so that he may give to one who pleases God. This, too, is vanity and chasing after the wind."*
>
> —Ecclesiastes 2:26 (AMP)

The Gordis translation of this is, *"Better joy in hand than the longing for distant pleasures."*

Wisdom, knowledge, and joy are what I consider to be some of the premium blessings of pleasing God. The sinner in the verse above chases after the wrong things in futility. His work and his efforts leave him devoid of what

God has intended to provide for him. It is God's pleasure to provide the joy we long for within our lives, as we follow Him. It's comforting to know that the joy of the Lord is our strength. This is a source of strength that manifests from the joy we receive as we walk with God. That is why it is imperative that we put our trust in Him every day.

> *"You make known to me the path of life;*
> *You will fill me with joy in Your presence,*
> *with eternal pleasures at Your right hand."*
>
> *—Psalm 16:11 (NIV)*

We may have the opportunity to experience moments of happiness based on situations or experiences that transpire in our lives. Joy is different. Joy is priceless, and it can't be bought with money. It comes from an understanding of who we are based on a relationship with Jesus. The joy of the Lord is our strength, and this joy is everlasting.

Going Beyond Skin-Deep

There are certain principles, laws of thought, and methodologies that may prove beneficial in certain areas of your life, yet they only go skin-deep. The wisdom that can only come from God, through His written word, is beyond comparison. The word of God can illuminate what is in your heart as you read it. It goes beyond skin-deep; it pierces through bone and marrow and the deepest parts of our nature, addressing what the Holy Spirit wants to reveal to us in our hearts.

"For the word of God is living and active and full of power [making it operative, energizing, and effective]. It is sharper

*than any two-edged sword, penetrating
as far as the division of the soul and spirit
[the completeness of a person], and of
both joints and marrow [the deepest parts
of our nature], exposing and judging the
very thoughts and intentions of the heart."*

–Hebrews 4:12 (AMP)

As we read and meditate on God's Word, it lightens up the path He wants our hearts and minds to follow.

*"Your word is a lamp to my feet
And a light to my path."*

–Psalm 119:105 (AMP)

Consuming a good cookie may bring delight. Consuming thirty trays of cookies in one setting will not bring a more delightful experience. This can also be true in our life choices; mass consumption of the same thing doesn't mean more delight. It could be quite the opposite.

Sometimes, we must test our activities or experiences to see and discern what is good. The Lord may show you other opportunities that can provide more value, significance, and internal reward, as you let Him lead you.

Let us be wise stewards of the time we have been given on Earth. Delight in the path that the Lord has set before you, and you will be blessed beyond measure.

Choose not to waste the precious seasons of life by collecting treasures or engaging in vain pursuits that do not provide a deep sense of delight within you. Only the Lord can truly provide this sense of continuous delight for you, as He delights in you following His path for your life!

"The steps of a [good and righteous] man are directed and established by the Lord,

And He delights in his way [and blesses his path]."

—Psalm 37:23 (AMP)

Chapter 6

YOUR BLESSED DESTINATION

"'For I know the plans and thoughts that I have for you,' says the Lord, 'plans for peace and well-being and not for disaster, to give you a future and a hope.'"

—Jeremiah 29:11 (AMP)

A
n appropriate acronym to remember and apply on your journey is F.M.T.P:

❑ **Faith:** God wants you to walk by faith as He leads you.

❑ **Mission:** God wants you to be on the mission to advance His kingdom.

❑ **Transition:** Allowing God to lead you in transition that may be necessary or required.

❑ **Provision:** God will supply and provide for your needs as you proceed by faith in His mission to advance the kingdom.

My hope and prayers are that you choose to follow Christ, so you can experience a real story of the extraordinary. Don't doubt Him; rather, trust Him with everything you have within you, and you will see a fruitful outcome.

Place first things first in your daily living. Make time at the beginning of your day to spend time with the Lord. Spend time reading the Bible, in meditation and in prayer. See the difference it makes when you place Him first, above all other priorities and objectives.

"I love those who love me;
And those who seek me early and
diligently will find me."

–Proverbs 8:17 (AMP)

Allow God to direct your plans as you seek Him and as He leads you down the path where you can experience the fruit He intends for your life. As you follow Him, He will cultivate the fruit inside you and "make firm" the plans He has for you.

"A man's mind plans his way [as he
journeys through life],
But the Lord directs his steps and
establishes them."

–Proverbs 16:9 (AMP)

Make your intention to "show up" every day, utilizing everything you have within you to live each day fully, as Christ lives in you and through you. May you experience every blessing and all the joy He has in store for you!

In Jesus' name,
Amen.

About the Author

Udi Umondak is passionate about empowering others. The insight provided through his customized resources will enable you to thrive in any area of life. Udi utilizes a comprehensive skill set that goes beyond coaching and motivational speaking. He is committed to helping others through his unique abilities discover and unleash their best to the world based on their God given identity and purpose.

You can find more resources available by the author at:

empowerinfinity.com

Printed in Great Britain
by Amazon

15745473R00058